edges of water

edges of water

Maureen Owen

chax
2013

ISBN 978-0-9894316-1-3

Chax Press
411 N Seventh Ave Ste 103
Tucson Arizona 85705-8388
USA

ACKNOWLEDGMENTS

Some of these poems have appeared in *Mipoesias, Bombay Gin* #32 & 34, *Court Green* #2 & #3, *Columbia Review* #18, *Talisman* #28-29, *Five Fingers Review* #22: *Uncanny Love, Thuggery & Grace* #4, *Shove* #2, *Uncontained, Square One* #4, *Left Hand Series* #11, *Belladonna* #100, *Visiting Wallace, The Recluse* #5, *Hanging Loose* #95, *The Poetry Show Anthology*, and *Fuzz Against Junk*.

On the cover: *Yellow Blue Center Fall*, by Elizabeth Murray.
Used with permission of the Murray-Holman Family Trust. With special thanks to Bob Holman.

For E.M

the subconscious is what you paint about

—Elizabeth Murray

Contents

"To model a moving interface, researchers conventionally have represented the boundary as a set of connected points–like a system of buoys loosely linked together with pieces of rope. The idea is to move each marker with the appropriate speed, according to the relevant equations of motion, and track the resulting changes in the interface's shape.

Such computational methods, however, often fail when the interface shape fluctuates rapidly, develops sharp corners or cusps, breaks up into smaller pieces, or merges with other features. In effect, the ropes connecting the buoys get tangled or severed."

–*Science News,* Vol 155, No. 15, p. 232
"Computing at the Edge," Ivars Peterson

to our foreheads   shaking

**poorly built ruckus of howling abstraction
or it could be dangerous for me to leave my sight**

three aboriginal women again   rowing a wood boat this time
my mother's house filling with water

long paddles stretching lazily over the wet gouache
at lake bottom a maze of finely painted hunting expeditions

smooth monster egg depiction of debris
floating dresses pink and slate of rosé

imagine dark torqued mermaids you won't see
they literally go crazy tattooed from cheap rents

spotless damp evening air lifting up an island
not an ocean   sky the color of elephants

these women glide sleek casual
not wearing continual explaining
not interfering with thinking

The indigo blue head scarf poem

for fanny

Make mine milk Wild Bill Elliot said
roaming through the tongue's secure motion

souls reborn in the body of bodies

                    the indigo blue head scarf
starts life drifting in   open water

now the bones of our fingers cover our eyes
patter over our ears   trawl air to uncover
what sense we are

surely we needn't go on slurping from these tin bowls
snow shovels   scraping at the ice   dealing with paper & loss

the Annunciation angel stands on her head
Ophelia has fashioned a straw   & coasts serenely

thoughts being intentions being feelings

the day has warmed
but   Is   this the address where we were supposed to show up?

in the photo the earth appears so far away
yet we are on it

Whales started small

blotches of verde

horse carrying in its teeth resilience   through black

when the circus barrier
was lifted   she ran
down across the
moor

   it was kind of liberating
but kind of crazy too

it was duplicated

deferred documentary

              crushed androgyny

Still   there are ways   if you were planning
to get   to heaven

stern and grey as brooding as stoves

a statue's restlessness embedded in the bedside table

with just enough crunch the others come and look at us

new tics in this crime

bouts-rimés sonnet

for Elizabeth Murray

give her some water to walk on

She's the lady with the ruby tucked in June
bathed in the meaning of stress
slightly askew in the seams of the moon
taffeta silken ochre & brazen with colors obsess-

ed by a motion so fancied in bracelets of snake
where the plans are as null as a number that's moot
she's the traveler akin to the loon on the cake
all have to agree in the air that was there stood a beaut

Bask in the glow of a true-to-life lantern sez Garbo
whispering puffs lather the nights of the play
put your finger in your eye and draw us a hobo
Nailed to the iris grape hyacinth periwinkle plaid of the day

O shivering orphan ice encased berry that's rhinestone
O hem of the brushed signature   salt tile her cologne

In the Valley of the Onions   or

Bebe

She was turning under her ceiling fan

I hung the bridle on a flathead nail   the whereabouts
in question   of mary magdelene   there were
a few wrinkles   Perched on a fig tree branch in the dim Garden of
Gethsemane?   In the kitchen during the Last Supper?   was she
painted out   fauxly bowdlerized?   She could take on anything   that
vast majority could throw at her   the very source of
these soi-disant Rental shoes   a scheme in contemplation

One night late   she carries home stars   through flooded streets
sections of a constellation wires & tubing   figures of the heavens
snagged
in the figures of speech

Oil slicks smear layering a turgid murk reflected color
around a golden sewer cover

Handbags in a tree

dour

or a spate of stuffed beasts and poisonous vapors (the morbid)

she stood in a pool of black water formed by the folds of her dress on the floor

Is it about   her malaise
it's not about concerning sky

it's not about going through a moment of
restrictive and mysterious skulls
it's certainly not about her collar of wolf fur interlaced
with provocative ribbons disclosing her

broodingly romantic streak   Darkness and the macabre
she was dancing cheek to cheek with fashion glossies
amid crystal and furnishings on a run away runway
Soon after most of them

tired of everything that formerly mattered
passed by eating tiny skeletons spun
from sugar   exiting a popular course
on the literature of horror

soon after   after her redress
bracelets of some leather dyed severly somber hues   with
bizarre & yellow beads sewn among the pewter
for who isn't cheered by a
vase full of ostrich feathers   at the end
of the day

"Tear it off! "

she had decided
she was releasing something against her

the folds of her dress on the floor formed a pool of black water where she stood

Blind   I see you
Putting on a show

       or identity hankers   to reign forever

In the gardener's house there is someone
entering the house of someone by that name
       entering the house of the garden

reconfigured in irregular suspensions   just behind the eyes
together out of passion we are warned

Standoffish things   invisible and swift
unsettling   as the things you dread

"Who knows how fat the devil is?"

       when mars was svelte
       a much denser jumble of rocks and dust came to visit

taut noises of the ballet' landings   like pepper falling in a shade
what goes awry can change behavior too

secretaries   poke their heads out
auguring

he'd said it wouldn't matter if it
came in 2's   or 3's
but out   beyond the grass line
light dimmed to spots where
she could only see the darkness

la negrura y la noche

the darkness and the night

shadowboxing

hear
sounds of   beads of   sweat   drying
make sorrow better

student w roaring leaf blower
strapped to her back
clears the brick path

      I am thinking   of difference

soft sweep of the broom
rush of straw on baked clay

When the sun goes down   I'll water the Yarrow

in yellow dark

Aborigines singing hopscotch   join   noisy night owls

Whatever was   on Mars   is gone now

he said I think my cheek hit the phone   much more

about the fabric than the gesture

wonder   about yourself

—Erik Satie

stare out at the sea for a   while longer
"Everyone wants a look"   dozens suggest

tatty silhouettes   &
only the sound of beads of sweat   drying

first the weight of history   then the weight
of the light   a warren of low blindfolding mist

where was I going when I got up
the police said they'd also found drugs in works of art

are you   listening to me?
are you feeling tense?

were you thinking about the icy membrane
50 miles above the surface   at the
edge of space

Beijing is built on dust

facing that bulk of scientific evidence

never keep a bottle more than 2 years
& never store it horizontally

craggy hills   often stretches of nothing
camels walking at moonlight   stop at every oasis

hand washed clothes   hang overhead

in the middle of the dream   they
went to another hotel   maybe
a schadenfreude (not ours) has taken hold maybe
the graph depicts fraudulent movement upscale
deviations maybe the hat an ancient flat-topped volcano
the tent a pyramid   the bad drawing of the fish   just that
maybe the baby rattle object rattles the 3 bending lines of vibration at one end
maybe tiny jellyfish human-faced octopi Stonehenge built of chicklets
maybe doodles define our pari passu with the states   all packed together so tightly
it's hard to know which one you're in   cluttered with
the scribblings   of bygone diners

Star-crossed ceramic lovers end it all
or scrubland

behold a great swath of the city's history
once a church then a mosque now   a museum
this happens to screetscapes   in the dead of winter
traffic comes back meaning Such a linguist!   who
insists on referring   to a shot of vodka

is it perilous to be wearing the pants of the remembered event
to be drawn into a maze of side streets   slick with packed
snow
vanished by brushes dunked in water

crunched bags of lovers dozens of them
joyous colored glazes rose and pink of
giant pairs of heads creating conversation

he had been that great a girlfriend

Ah to see the big wigs in their big boats

the sad faces of Hollywood in the checkout line

ambient

        or blister chic

I sprinkled the salt over the patches of ice where you
fell   under the influence of the vague dialogue hissing
through the holes   under your hair

she could hear the lights from the Hershey Bars

Pausing despite the relaxed capitals
refusing to stand still even for a second among the tourist infested stalls
not one but two sequined shirts

a lone Brazil nut tree
sometimes a nut collapses
if you're not left unconscious
this difference doubles for evidence

who stands up   to sit down
a body of water   much dissected but never completely explained
because we cannot fully see into it
the way the child sees into herself   a study in minimalism a
tiny box with bare walls and concrete floors

can you turn the pages fast enough
to escape from the contents

perforated with apertures for archers
in coffee and carpet shops

Afghan is ta n
shelled, bullet-pocked buildings
patched back together after being hammered into fragments
the artifacts

ordinary rhythms of life
around a wobbling barrel

the situation stumped by our distraction of shopping
our own private serape-topped beach chairs

intending argument circumnavigated at an alarming rate
while all the vocalists headed back to the car

as always in a rush   their mango crème brûlée untouched

it's wise to wear beige

for who the tip of survival of the honeymoon
no bed of daisies yawning   sites of caveat
recall fire in the lenga trees

charred melee

created from local materials   like dirt

or visitors sometimes wept   on the bedroom threshold

a mother with a young child took a quick nap
elderly women clustered on concrete benches overlooking the water

I miscalculated I was looking   at you Miss   I missed
science and the mood of darkness I missed statistics
chartreuse volcanic stumps   I parked the car in a pond

several people can't recall the name they were born with
they've had so many names
their own true name
an unknown situation
an invigorating tension swathed in dark blankets   with
woolen eyes

embossed of icy remains
a motor shuffles
deciding which of the night's dozens of parties to forgo

because when others were taking the stars apart
I was trying to put together some kind of organized sense of existence   I'd
because I didn't wish you were still that person I could recognize

because Flannery O'Connor couldn't climb the stairs
7 tall white rockers on the veranda

**you could drive for hours along its crumbling cliffs and not pass
a single car**

for Jenny Dorn

Was it the level of the mighty rocks
compromised by the shattering of
the pirates that rose and fell
into the depths of
A giant Vuitton logo made of fire extinguisher red gerber daisies erected in
that center of her discouragement

for the upwardly mobile nothing signals arrival like luxury brands
shipped across the sea today as dollars inundating China

She was so full of a sense of loss from before
and knowing the multimedia loss resembled she had no simple
words and when she looked no real hardware of what
it could be   they could not get the
FEMA map to fit inside the FEMA trailer   what is the
fascination with a severed head   a severed head resting among old shoes
this was the predicament of her understanding
a lot of people who have embraced indulgence today are first-timers

If I could rinse my hair in
seawater salt it would be curly again
She knows what she remembers
that the sun slides from the sheering

the trouble had been   that she had her back to
everything in the room

29

wrong number on my cell phone
   "Hey Speedy
      this is Walkin' callin'
   This is the last shot
   you got!"

      or   when the moon breaks down   and demons pass the salt

she moved
the light moved   celestial bodies changed addresses in sky geographies &
the pumping of the heart   so moved   certain hormones & molecules of being
mosey in days later   another moved before   who kept an actual sheep &
lugged great bags of smelly wool to the local p. o.   a spiritual journey for the wool   a
peacock damsel in laced corset   fleeing all those statements heard   that
seemed so important just last week   so if the oracle shows up in a vase of flowers
spreads her tall chrysanthemum arms
offering   sweet lady luck
bliss   felicity & such
speak up for what you want and need   & of a move so made
while you were at a table writing
As for myself
happiness causes me to panic
seized by thoughts of tragic problems I'm neglecting   by
being happy   & so consumed I'm moving again   back in time to aid
those loved that I'd let down   Why endure the consequences of the past? a man
returns home from a party   tosses his top hat on a hall stand where a candle
left lit for him   sets it on fire   Jefferson remarked
his preference for american women content with "the
tender and tranquil amusements of domestic life"   not meddling   not meddling
in politics as their Parisian counterparts a man comes home candlelight sets his hat
on fire
Now it's 2 a.m. out in the dark
a full standing portrait
of the heiress   attired in brocade and lace   holds two
large Caribbean kitchen knives   & thanks the group
from the bottom of her heart

which reminds me
do you want to buy
tickets to the marriage
of Figuro

Rarely discuss in public   the Persian blue hair
disappeared into the thin   distraction   the perfume
of motion   once your plane
crashes into the open sea
first of all there's no need to panic (most of the time)
Do not fish
Remain perpendicular to the turquoise border at
the bottom of the sky   Gaudy delusions
of fabulous glamour white washed stucco cabanas
set above a coral reef
as close to the water as they can be without floating away
earth-red Mexican tile floors
dining room open to some of the best snorkeling on the coast
what I have pieced together   combing my hairbrush

**after
the air of their leaving brushed back
upon us**

the Maya designed a pyramid   the
eerie remains of an abandoned club so
that at times the setting sun casts a
moving shadow   it resembles a serpent
slithering down the northern staircase.
Most striking during the Equinox
the snow was slowly drifting off the wicker porch chairs
an undulating ceiling   draped across the wing shaped beams
the only downside   which goes only as far as
the luscious red fiberglass panels of its soaring roof reflect the
hubbub of urban life   into the interior patio
warm shades of tobacco chocolate and pewter

but now   the out islands   are in

uncanny love / a love elegy

distracted by the perfume   of her motion

All the roses skidding   down
her skirt a terrible lushness of flamingo   when she moves a thick
green humming in the stems a sound that mocks the sound
that running water makes in the desert that sounds like people
talking   a murmurous cistern ruckus that flees
those loose flowing satin dresses while completely unconstructed her
knees
define a fishtail silhouette
wonders   of a dreaming swarm where we lay prone
and snoring   a simulacrum of our mysterious
motivations glittering beadwork yeh yeh   O O baby
patiently forming
out of the ill lit saturation
all typically, intangibly Rio
tho every night is a party night in Bombay
it's never this crowded in Delhi   where
we danced in moonlight on bare planks   there

33

Taped to the dawn
or tiny silver bridge

No trees are falling now   Where no stalagmitic sprout
under frozen pipes   No pantry disasters
voo doo water spurt   faucets solidly locked in ice   to get into the
self-help thing late at night   to have never been to Paris   that
conditional nature of exposure where the lip gloss in the ad   is
christened
Scarlet Fever   No wood burning stove conflagration
to get there just in time   tho left in some sense wounded   no drafts
pour in   around the windows' frame   a neighbor practices her singing
in
a high raw trill of ascending blue ice to not to want her to stop   to go
into the room
closest to her voice   no cracked panes   no holes
in the floor

            Dear Junior,
            Thank you for loaning me your smith-corona
            typewriter   with 3 fortune cookie fortunes
            taped to the left of the carriage

            You will never need to worry about a steady income.
            Don't let friends impose on you, work calmly and
silently.
            You will be successful in your work.

                                no gaps

no winter hazard warnings No furnace failure   washing machine
cold water hoses split
Don't stop   Don't stop singing   go
into the room closest to her voice   no trees
no trees
no trees
no trees are falling now

Niedecker Calendar Poem

Last Year or "backwards to its source"

January 2003

Behold the fields of white
as if a milk fed westerner
come home.

February 2003

'Twixt town and country
I'm just plain Ms—
between the seams
fashion loves a prodigy.

March 2003

When the elephant
comes in for a drink
it makes so much
noise and
destroys everything.

April   2003

A far-fetched theory is far
fetched.
It dawned
perfectly complementing the neon-
hued hairdos—
You said you were there in Coco.

May   2003

The cognoscenti prance about
the planetary
print over a chiffon dress
voices nip at my heels.

June   2003

While Rubens delighted in
play of light and dim
nothing seemed to fit at its peak—
a source of menace and wonder populated
by tremulous.

July   2003

grass too high
by the lake
blows flat
best illustrated.

August   2003

You could get lost in those
flowering tresses—
a supreme cause of
linear procession
but I had too many bruises.

September 2003

Boards painted with cream
Nor do they necessarily mean
what they seem to say
I am postponed by
choice before.

October 2003   .

There is a sense here that
the deceased still linger—
tweed knickered the sisters
preferred his versions.

November 2003

A shift from the
ideals of thrift
the fit of the upholstery
just wraps around you.

December 2003

Shadows blew through
the trees.

just another rigid silhouette
              emerging from a taxidermist's studio
   or

Threaded about the swoop

Heard about the bird flu threat (epidemic) having
second thoughts about her vacation
Maybe I'm chicken she said   but
I'd rather play it safe

Held about the head bud sacrificing
pollen orphans about her chapels
forgiveme eyes wing'ed her rattled   between
she'd surely bowl those   birds

Why   that day
except that in it we took a walk
                    by a choking ocean

probably invisible to be lavishly on looks
anything in me slowly at times

thatch & guzzle shrine to pine   sea-grass   &sand
migratorious   dabbling in the heroine's toils

                    should   you get to live
another life

sand blowing from your teeth

ad nauseam tranquility of strangers
blousy   bones   Without
chromosome

it's hotter than blazes   she said

What made the scholar holler
Was her love of Mozambique

Ornate Moorish squiggles   scoot gab   notch

                                            sidereal

spotted pint-sized fancies
unescorted

bodies of humbler folks tucked in wall niches now empty

no one   in the freezer

now   you are everywhere   like the light

what's hard to miss plenteous is the question   writing

nature of a witness attached to the word

gangling   large and small

instead

"Other artists paint a bridge, a house, a boat...
I want to paint the air that surrounds the bridge,
the house, the boat: the beauty of the air."
—C. Monet

...the beauty of the air   So tonic draught intensity a liquid   or

when you were dead

will I still always   be here

a dream still feeling like a dream   tiny ruined hotels

hushed

        sleek luxury bruised   bring along some food to plant   on
balconies
adrift

starving and broke   groups with ankles   plummeted

children from the beach the sheer number of sheer fabrics

ever did

sequins unburden cliché on a clear top
hanging screens sort of liberate the hors d'oeuvres
Ralph Lauren buys sunglasses

and none of it sheds light on air travel

these troubled   waters   & sugar
your situation

a pale horse grazes yellow grass
between stacks of black tires

The Princess of New Mexico will see you now

Not a triptych

not an accidental

    scrambled on a wrinkled

      wind hits the screen like break-ins
Such a lilt as light on previous   glow its folly
cacti snared the Baedeker   captivating ly
grabbed here and snatched there   everyone holding up their
drinks
I saw the face of Puss in Boots
the look on the face of Puss in Boots   coiffed yachts of sweet nights
shiftless adverbs   in their palace

**my neighbors relax on their flat southwest porch
chatting in Spanish   Just
like I always wanted my neighbors to do**

Christian monasteries and Ottoman mosques

or   there arrives the fitful pinched

dotted with ruins curving surging chalkiness of swirls and dabs endlessly
torsos
and buckling circling mud-caked walls
splender and solitude the size of a roaring waterfall   stuffed
            through rough sluices of limestone and shale

compared to   their approach

the sound of real string beans snapping
                        punish the dense and the glamorous

what happened was I sat   in a different chair
fringing the shoppers' bulky sleeves
    at sale   riotous messy and   so fragile

                            breathe stuttered rows
                            leafy   & a grand piano

to you I hail   Look

Gustave Courbet has put the bend in the river
directly in the center of his painting

he grew up there   tho not as a young man

in all   Loose surroundings which boil

untroubled a girl turns her head in a field of flax   lights fling out from
her auburn hair   over acres of tiny blue flowers

   O   she says   I dance   as a dancer

the lioness   with a cacophonous fan

or learning noise

that same person over and over
who we are   in defiance of fools
sleeping in wisteria

straw yellow sand &
                            3 olive jars
ochre stucco wall   half on its hair   fire tiles!

I am untouched as by a swath of Patagonia!

painted with heavy cream   thick plank side boards
Rigorous White

                              the tremendous weight of the afternoon

in sculpted trees   in arcs of iris
in continuous solar downpour   an inexplicable language
moans to me over the tangled inflections   perfuming

this air   along this exuberant boulevard

Just to be moving   a wrinkle in the inscrutable   a

camouflage of normality   Luck is so full of mischief

   & the banshee trains shriek through   on their scheduled hours

losing our sense of nostalgia

or

exploding houses

the vaulted ceilings
blue-skinned goddesses inanely buoyant
pink-peach plaster trimmed in white

he said you won't be asked to leave   but you will want to leave
In the woods of language   I
white wash   & thistle shadow
inflating
and deflating

everything depends on who's dancing
she had come to the leaf quite late

just when the blue irises the yellow roses and the red roses from Kansas
bloomed full out in the yard

the thieves stole the copper piping   w/out
shutting off the gas

for George

howled and trilling

Will there be rapids?

or   **a fava bean shaped pool**

he mailed the year straight unto the tongue

At 9 in the coffee bean forest
clothes hung in the air on the glass manikins

clothes you can't go anywhere in

filled with people working

millions of teacups of rain   came down in torrents
clustering traits harpsichordist   it's all like high heels
kept in one place
rendering   faithfully   the noise alone

not surprisingly what we have   often very personal elements
speak carbonated pendulum   so many cross over
not knowing where it comes from

after others before us

for Katie

Haiku for George Schneeman

the last calendar
our artist sailed away
hangs in my kitchen

she rarely   took the bridge   *a pantoum*
                                              for the Minnesota bridge collapse
disaster

lens flares or   the reflection of her flesh off the dust in the air
of pouring whistled white and curving   forms   formlessness
that each of us forms to our own conspires
whosoever placed them placed them there in places

of pouring whistled white and curving   forms   formlessness
that were already   vanishing
whosoever placed them placed them there in places
a robbery occurred   camouflaged by the middle of the day

that were already   vanishing
distant hills poured into the woods
a robbery occurred   camouflaged by the middle of the day
the spiritual tour guide was an ex Xerox salesman

distant hills poured into the woods
ideas best understood as an extreme on the continuum
the spiritual tour guide was an ex Xerox salesman
pitch black latticed with gaps where   she

ideas best understood as an extreme on the continuum
into that charged air that defined her immovable presence
pitch black latticed with gaps where   she
rarely   took   the bridge

people more like they actually are
that each of us forms to our own conspires
if she'd had a choice she might not have chosen
lens flares or   the reflection of her flesh off the dust in the air

**flowered napkins thrown over baseball caps Lawrence of Arabia style
riding double on the pinto rocking horse   chanting**

> *We are weirdoes traveling in a weird world.*
> —Benjamin and Jacob ages 6 and 4

Consider the skipping

> *for Wallace Stevens after* Anecdote of the Jar

people took leave of their senses
a sort of place fold in time
Makeshift bouquets of wild palms
bashful paintings poking out of the back of a getaway van

hotel walls of salt block   the moon would
ascend next to a layer of thick white salt
Whiteness flats wash planetary
alien evaporated hymnal in its rising

such backdrop into which we dump
our charged iris   eyeballed by Milky Way
latticed spiked   fringed by a space
all its own

are we effected adversely   by living on a magnet

or liquid
          mercury of alchemy   **spreading**

skin porous as seeing through ornate walls

imagine a Bonnard and a Vermeer in these empty frames
of thoughts   teetering on the arms of our chairs
we're all the same   in different ways
the bronze noses of the guardian statues (lion) (equestrian)
eyebrows suspended in midair   boughs over an ancient road

the sculpture under his bed for years
I
hope you don't mind us yelling   "the
toilets exploded!"
                teetering

thoughts on the arms of chairs
boughs like eyebrows over the ancient road
about the same or   similar
Bobolinks called skunk blackbirds in some places

the sternness of your features

He said "Hello Dad"   then he could not talk
Not in-person call in a video conference call   so boy
so overcome he clutched   clumsy receiver to ear   staring at big black
box television screen

after a perfect storm the need to find a perfect house
Skinny   but sturdy little homes
tin roofs small porches   colored like Easter eggs on wheels
rose-hip pink   malted mint   cloudless blue   ceiling fans   beds a table and
chairs

nothing washes down the lasagna layered with cashew ricotta quite like a
          tarragon and tonic

I
hope you don't mind us yelling   "the
toilets exploded!"

almost alone among   sponge-washed walls

for Lorine Niedecker

Lorine threw the dish at the door

That couldn't have been

          Seagulls   long
before   I ever   saw the sea

"yikes yikes" dogs bark

to be at your feet
will never be the same they say

unhinged but intact

vacuumed   not just in the ripping
you occupy

throwed in the weeds
screaming "she looked like most of her style!"

nothing ever rouses the mango trees

55

rough boys carried the lilacs in

splashed with mud by a passing taxi
eating from new patterns and hues
banditod   steep tufty hillsides

in the 4 degree night

visit me from the incident   whistling shade
eerie ceremony mystery   pagan   spooky
can quietly   into its traverse

a
conjugation of the dead:

I dead	we dead
you (familiar) dead	you all dead
he she it dead	they dead

no matter no matter   the night's still young!

Don't worry if you can't salsa!
those uneven   come to know so much about it
         you will want to get off the roadside

O then   bring layers

antecedently

by previously
born from

before

If we walk into a restaurant
If we're a   humbling/curvilinear location   filtering substance &
quintessence

if we in slangy   spotted tufting
calibrate to be on fire   jittering   to influence chatter

spliced prior

we think we look back
we just look outside   surface that is a state

of meringue

holiness that is a condition   independent
of deity

when recalling stark
whatnot efforts   /anomie

tethered

the thing that strikes us is the distance
while the dog appears indifferent to the art on the walls

it's some pool
assembled by water

milk stretch limo stretch of coast line
parked in front of my house

bouts-rimés sonnet II

when hair grew out of your head

Ridden with crime marred by graffiti June
when the art object fails to evaporate stress
who can't afford not to change with the moon?
tho my parents fretted I would obsess

But unless their feet are pumping it's not the snake
outsiders strode nonchalance their way across moot
to fit the lid for storing we smashed the blue frosting cake
lazy afternoons reflected in the clouds insufferable beaut

She was hard to disentangle from the shadows so Garbo
take the case of artists and their ability to express play
they tore back the train tracks from every small depot's hobo
Was it happening again between Paris and New York's day?

Was shopping for a toolbox a shout-out against rhinestone
romance and the pressures of cologne?

Disease plague accident or epidemic

for bush & chaney

Two moguls of power
One bent forward
forming a walrus shape
The other picaresquely waving a
fin over the walrus

**Drunkenness   became widespread among the enlisted troops   sent
to quell   the   Whiskey Rebellion**
                              or the state of the union

overstuffed suitcases Clouds lug through a
sky frayed couch slip covered in moss
rose to adjust rectangular time

the mechanical arm nuzzles Martian dust when
she stands to accept the award   the top
buttons of her dress pop off   gripping her chest

she faces   the packed house   a
summer twilight sitting with a deaf woman shelling peas
hesitation was not a support   but a reference point
yonder came the feeding frenzy   nations for life

What are you thinking now
The captured dictator is not himself
Can a remark be proven by reason of
scarred surfaces

Ash settling into the front yard
Foothills on fire

the future of memory

the future takes just the shadow of the giraffe
the path of the neck under dotted swiss

turnips boiling in interrupted   bars of
golden boxcars of shafts of sunlight

sped over the rails through the country
A train leaping the tracks & heading

out across the flat prairie to a
small cabin in extreme   cowboy boots

& leather cows and steers & goats   &
luggage   we pack to journey

to a destination we have no memory of
or care to stage in terms of a past

just the shadow of someone's chin line
in an August sunset against

cliffs & quilted sand dunes
stove pipes   humming

we have become birds

lost luggage

my car had almost stopped itching
all the red dots
dissolved into my skin
I lost my luggage   in the snow
acres of blizzard
we were in the driveway   don't look back
someone said   and that was how   I
lost my luggage

A Wake for the WTC

Outside   in the dark
not the robust sounds of summer
but   September's insects
softly purring
subdued music
holding one long chirp
one prolonged chirp
holding one long rolling chirp
it's broken bits
rising as one long steady chant
a litany of sound
and the sound becomes the sound
of the names of the dead
tender xeroxed signs (flyers) with photos
fluttering along the fenses of union square
and the sound of the sound
is the names of the dead

And the sound becomes the sound
of the names of the dead

Jenny's Garden

Iris leaves no flowers   Cosmos
tall   coneflower
lambs ears
portulaca in a clay pot
daisy
sunflower
jimson weed still furled
green apples   grape vines
w/purpled grapes
Pennsylvania smartweed
sea lavendar
holly hock
what white 5 petaled was it?
not petunia   but
Black eyed-Susan
old world roses   facing
Aztec spirit head
red flower that hangs down
small pine

Cricket   katydid   Cicada

Tuvan throat songs

american dark

About The Author

Maureen Owen currently in Denver, Colorado, is the author of ten poetry titles, most recently *Erosion's Pull* from Coffee House Press. *Erosion's Pull* was a finalist for the Colorado Book Award and the Balcones Poetry Prize. She currently teaches at Naropa University, both on campus and in the low-residency MFA Creative Writing Program, and is editor-in-chief of Naropa's on-line zine *not enough night*. She can be found reading her work on the PennSound website.

About Chax Press

Chax Press is a 501(c)(3) nonprofit organization, founded in 1984, and has published more than 140 books, including fine art and trade editions of literature and book arts works.

For more information, please see our web site at *http://chax.org*

Chax Press is supported by individual contributions, and by the Tucson Pima Art Council and the Arizona Commision on the Arts, with funds from the State of Arizona and the National Endowment for the Arts. Particular thanks to this book go to the 117 individual donors to our 2013 Kickstarter campaign, of which this book is the third publication to be issued.

TUCSON PIMA
ARTS
COUNCIL

Arizona
Commission
on the Arts

NATIONAL
ENDOWMENT
FOR THE ARTS